First World War
and Army of Occupation
War Diary
France, Belgium and Germany

2 DIVISION
19 Infantry Brigade,
Brigade Supply Column
20 August 1914 - 20 August 1915

WO95/1367/4

The Naval & Military Press Ltd
www.nmarchive.com
Published in association with The National Archives

Published by

The Naval & Military Press Ltd

Unit 10 Ridgewood Industrial Park,

Uckfield, East Sussex,

TN22 5QE England

Tel: +44 (0) 1825 749494

www.naval-military-press.com

www.nmarchive.com

This diary has been reprinted in facsimile from the original. Any imperfections are inevitably reproduced and the quality may fall short of modern type and cartographic standards.

© **Crown Copyright**
Images reproduced by permission of The National Archives, London, England, 2015.

Contents

Document type	Place/Title	Date From	Date To
Heading	WO95/1367 19th Inf Bde Supply Column		
Heading	19th Inf. Bde Supply Column 1914 Aug-1915 Aug.		
Heading	19th Brigade Supply Column Vols. I. II & III 20.8-31.10.14.		
War Diary	Amiens	20/08/1914	20/08/1914
War Diary	Valenciennes	21/08/1914	23/08/1914
War Diary	Le Cateau	24/08/1914	24/08/1914
War Diary	Le Forest	25/08/1914	25/08/1914
War Diary	Bapaume	26/08/1914	26/08/1914
War Diary	Siquentin	27/08/1914	27/08/1914
War Diary	Noyon	28/08/1914	28/08/1914
War Diary	Compeigne	29/08/1914	29/08/1914
War Diary	Senlis	30/08/1914	01/09/1914
War Diary	St Mard	02/09/1914	02/09/1914
War Diary	La Borget	03/09/1914	03/09/1914
War Diary	Chaiume	04/09/1914	04/09/1914
War Diary	Lieusaint	05/09/1914	05/09/1914
War Diary	Brunoy	06/09/1914	07/09/1914
War Diary	Tournan	08/09/1914	09/09/1914
War Diary	Couloummiers	10/09/1914	10/09/1914
War Diary	Dhuisy	11/09/1914	11/09/1914
War Diary	Couloummiers	12/09/1914	12/09/1914
War Diary	Nevilly St Front	13/09/1914	26/09/1914
War Diary	Neville	27/09/1914	06/10/1914
War Diary	Crepy	07/10/1914	08/10/1914
War Diary	Travelling All Night	09/10/1914	09/10/1914
War Diary	Montreuil	10/10/1914	10/10/1914
War Diary	St Omer	11/10/1914	11/10/1914
War Diary	Lumbres	12/10/1914	12/10/1914
War Diary	Hazebruck	13/10/1914	13/10/1914
War Diary	Thiennes	14/10/1914	15/10/1914
War Diary	Vlamertinghe	16/10/1914	17/10/1914
War Diary	Caestre	18/10/1914	19/10/1914
War Diary	Merville	20/10/1914	23/10/1914
War Diary	Inclusive	24/10/1914	31/10/1914
Heading	19th Bde Supply Column Vol IV 1-30.11.14		
War Diary		01/11/1914	30/11/1914
Heading	19th Bde Supply Col Vol V 1-31.12.14.		
War Diary	Nieppe	30/12/1914	31/12/1914
War Diary	Nieppe	26/12/1914	29/12/1914
War Diary	Nieppe	23/12/1914	25/12/1914
War Diary	Nieppe	19/12/1914	22/12/1914
War Diary	Nieppe	14/12/1914	18/12/1914
War Diary	Nieppe	10/12/1914	13/12/1914
War Diary	La Creche	05/12/1914	05/12/1914
War Diary	Nieppe	06/12/1914	09/12/1914
War Diary	La Creche	01/12/1914	04/12/1914
War Diary	19th Brigade-Supply Col Vol VI 1-31.1.15.		
War Diary	Nieppe	01/01/1915	31/01/1915

Heading	19th Brigade Supply Coln Vols VII, VIII, IX 6.2-30.4.15		
Heading	February 1915. 19th July Bde Supply Column.		
War Diary	Nieppe	06/02/1915	28/02/1915
War Diary	March 1915. 19th Inf. Bde Supply Column.		
War Diary	Nieppe	01/03/1915	31/03/1915
Heading	April 1915 19th July Bde Supply Column		
War Diary	Nieppe	01/04/1915	30/04/1915
Heading	19th Bde Supply Col? Vol X		
Heading	War Diary 19th Inf Bde Supply Column May-1915.		
War Diary	Nieppe	01/05/1915	19/05/1915
War Diary	Armentieres	20/05/1915	31/05/1915
Heading	27th Division 19th Infy Bde 19th Bde Supply Coln. Jun-July 1915.		
Heading	19th Bde Supply Coln Vol XI		
Heading	19th Inf. Bde Supply Column		
War Diary	Armentieres	01/06/1915	30/06/1915
Heading	19th Brigade Supply Coln Vol XII.		
Heading	War Diary of 19th Inf. Bde. Supply Column.		
War Diary	Armentieres	01/07/1915	14/07/1915
War Diary	Steen Werk	15/07/1915	21/07/1915
War Diary	Doulieu	22/07/1915	31/07/1915
Heading	19th Brigade Supply Coln Vol XIII From 1st to 20th August 1915		
War Diary	Doulieu	01/08/1915	18/08/1915
War Diary	St Omer	19/08/1915	20/08/1915

WO 95/1367

14th Inf Bde Supply Colum

19th Inf. Bde
Supply Column
~~Aug - Dec 1914~~

1914 AUG — 1915 AUG

Aug 5/6

121/2/65

19th Brigade Supply Column

Vols. I, II & III   20.8 — 31.10.14

WAR DIARY or INTELLIGENCE SUMMARY

Army Form C. 2118.

Hour, Date, Place	Summary of Events and Information	Remarks and References to Appendices
20th August 1914 AMIENS	Received orders from A.D.S.T. to form a XIX Brigade Supply Column consisting of 7 Lorries (3 Ton) manned army & petrol lorries, motor bicycle, taken from 0r IV Divl Supply Column. Column formed ready for marching at 8 p.m. Also rendezvous of A.D.S.T. Received orders with direction of march. Also 1 Motor car (Ford) issued. of XIX Bde Train with 1 N.g. & 3 other ranks of supply section.	
21st August VALENCIENNES	Left AMIENS at 6.30 am arrived at VALENCIENNES at 6 am accompanied by Lieut Brocade MURRAY who reported to Ad.gun.gH the Train. Deposited personally Senior R.T.O was informed that the Train would arrive at 17 on 22nd at MARBY station. Bivouacked for the night at VALENCIENNES.	
22nd August VALENCIENNES	Reported to Capt A. CLIFTON SHELTON Comdg XIX Bde Train at 7 am. Handed over Cars & Supply Details. Received information that rail lines at SOLESMES where N.C.Os to pick up 2 days supplies. Proceeded to SOLESMES & loaded supplies all except 1 day's Hay and 1 day's Oats. Delivered Supplies for 3 Regt at QUIÉVRECHAIN; 1Regt (R.W.F) at OMMAING. Returned to SOLESMES picked up supplies remaining & marched to VALENCIENNES at 1 am. Bivouacked.

Army Form C. 2118.

WAR DIARY
or
INTELLIGENCE SUMMARY.
(Erase heading not required.)

Instructions regarding War Diaries and Intelligence Summaries are contained in F. S. Regs., Part II. and the Staff Manual respectively. Title pages will be prepared in manuscript.

Hour, Date, Place	Summary of Events and Information	Remarks and References to Appendices
23rd August 1914. VALENCIENNES.	Arrived at QUIEVRECHAIN at 6am dumped supplies. Returned to SOLESMES still railhead, preferred to VALENCIENNES as Rendezvous.	
24th August 1914. LE CATEAU.	Reached LE CATEAU filled & went to LE FOREST as Rendezvous, 4 pm got orders from Brigade HQrs and reported to G.H.Q. twice. About to return for instructions at 6 am, but foremen at LE FOREST.	
25th August 1914. LE FOREST.	Reported to G.H.Q. at 6am received orders to proceed to CAMBRAI and dump supplies returning, reached at LANDIGNY. Spanned day, night searching for Brigade finally located them at LE CATEAU at 2am 25th. "	
26th August 1914. BAPAUME.	Refilled at MARITZ. Returned to Railhead BAPAUME & got orders to proceed to ESTREY there deliver food to any horse requiring it all night at ESTREY. "	

Forms/C. 2118/10.

Army Form C. 2118.

WAR DIARY
or
INTELLIGENCE SUMMARY.
(Erase heading not required.)

Instructions regarding War Diaries and Intelligence Summaries are contained in F. S. Regs., Part II. and the Staff Manual respectively. Title pages will be prepared in manuscript.

Hour, Date, Place	Summary of Events and Information	Remarks and References to Appendices
27 August 1914. ST QUENTIN	Reached ST QUENTIN. Received exit without orders from Brigade HdQrs. Brigade hurrying through. Located Brigade in direction of CHAUNY. Supplied troops with food.	
28 August 1914. NOYON.	Starting retiring in rear of 3rd Division at 4 am. Reached NOYON. Refilled at PONT OISE. Returned to new Railhead COMPEIGNE.	
29 August 1914. COMPEIGNE.	Refilled at CARLEPONT & returned to railhead. (COMPEIGNE).	
30 August 1914. SENLIS.	New railhead PONT ST MAXENCE. Lorry up supplied from COULOISY. Proceeded to new railhead at SENLIS.	
31 August 1914. SENLIS.	Loaded and awaited orders all day. At 11 p.m. received a telephone message that Brigade were at Railway Crossing at VERBERIE. Proceeded there arriving at about 2 a.m. No rose up or sign of Train. Finally at dawn wind up in side road away, unshipped a loose wall, close to * VERBERIE without repetting.	* from an officer who was up to coup of

V. R. September 1914
VERBERIE

WAR DIARY
or
INTELLIGENCE SUMMARY.
(Erase heading not required.)

Army Form C. 2118.

Instructions regarding War Diaries and Intelligence Summaries are contained in F. S. Regs, Part II. and the Staff Manual respectively. Title pages will be prepared in manuscript.

Hour, Date, Place	Summary of Events and Information	Remarks and References to Appendices
1st September 1914. SENLIS.	Returned to SENLIS where orders were received to proceed to BARRON to Refill. New Railhead ST MARD. Refilled against BARRON	
2nd September 1914. ST MARD	Railhead ST MARD. Refilled at DAMARTIN Started for new Railhead at 10 p.m.	
3rd September 1914. LE BOURGET	Railhead LE BOURGET. Refilled at CLAIGNY.	
4th September 1914. CHAUME.	Railhead CHAUME. Refilled at TOSSIGNY and returned to TOURNAN.	
5th September 1914. LIEUSAINT.	Railhead LIEUSAINT. Refilling from GRISY.	
6th September 1914. BRUNOY.	Railhead at LIEUSAINT but received orders to proceed to OUR CORANT & load up from Reserve Park. Refilled at OZOIR la FERRIÈRE. Returning to Railhead at BRUNOY.	
7th September 1914. BRUNOY.	Left BRUNOY full at 6 am refilled at VILLENEUVE S' DENIS. returned to BRUNOY.	
8th September 1914. TOURNAN.	Railhead TOURNAN. Refilling from PIERRE LEVÉE.	

Army Form C. 2118.

WAR DIARY
or
INTELLIGENCE SUMMARY
(Erase heading not required.)

Instructions regarding War Diaries and Intelligence Summaries are contained in F. S. Regs., Part II. and the Staff Manual respectively. Title pages will be prepared in manuscript.

Hour, Date, Place	Summary of Events and Information	Remarks and References to Appendices
9th September 1914.	Reached MONTCERF repelled at PIERRE LEVEE.	
10th September 1914. COULOMMIERS.	Reached COULOMMIERS. Proceeded towards REBAIS but was not allowed to go farther. Being unsafe, Lorry Lorries returned to GUILLERS.	
11th September 1914. DOUISY.	Proceeded meeting rear of STCRY & MERY generally repelled. Brigade at point 209 near COCHEREL. Bivouac at DOUISY.	
12th September 1914. COULOMMIERS.	Returned to COULOMMIERS early & repelled at MARIZY ST GENEVIEVE, returned again to COULOMMIERS; moved out night and rain fell, reached Railhead at 12 midnight loaded & reached STCRY at 4 am.	
13th September 1914. NEUILLY ST FRONT.	Reached detraining point at BUZANCY. Railways covered & carried them to G.H.Q at FERE EN TARDENOIS bivouac at NEUILLY ST FRONT on road to MONNES to Courson a Reserve Park.	
14th September 1914. NEUILLY ST FRONT.	Reloaded at MONNES repelled train at SEPTMONTS. Returned to NEUILLY.	
15th September 1914.	Reloaded at NEUILLY Repelled at SEPTMONTS.	
16th September 1914. to 18th September 1914.	Railhead at NEUILLY Repelled at SEPTMONTS.	
inclusive.

Army Form C. 2118.

WAR DIARY
or
INTELLIGENCE SUMMARY.
(Erase heading not required.)

Instructions regarding War Diaries and Intelligence Summaries are contained in F. S. Regs., Part II. and the Staff Manual respectively. Title pages will be prepared in manuscript.

Hour, Date, Place	Summary of Events and Information	Remarks and references to Appendices
19 September 1914 to 26 September 1914 inclusive	Railhead ordered at NEUILLY as for 3rd Corps but supplies were drawn at OUCHY-SOUS-BRENY under 2nd Corps Ordnance Stores to Men at NEUILLY. ✱ On 26th drew an extra days rations from O.H.Q. Lorries received at HARTENNES Refilling point at SEPTMONT.	
27 September 1914. NEUILLY.	Same Railhead & refilling point. (NEUILLY & SEPTMONTS.)	
28 September 1914	Same Railhead & refilling point. Ordnance Stores for R.W.F. Lorry returned to base	
29 September 1914	Same Railhead & refilling point.	
30 September 1914.	Same Railhead & refilling point. Letter to O.H.Q. for 2nd Ordnance Lorry. Also reporting no supplies kept at any time.	

Army Form C. 2118.

WAR DIARY
or
~~INTELLIGENCE SUMMARY.~~
(Erase heading not required.)

Instructions regarding War Diaries and Intelligence Summaries are contained in F.S. Regs., Part II. and the Staff Manual respectively. Title pages will be prepared in manuscript.

Hour, Date, Place	Summary of Events and Information	Remarks and references to Appendices
1st October 1914. to 5th October 1914	NEVILLY. Reached & ~~Sept~~ repelling paint Repair general overhauls to lorries at SEPTMONT.	carried out.
6th October 1914. NEVILLY	Reached PUCHY BRENY. Refilled at St REMY.	
7th October 1914. ~~CREPY~~ CREPY	Reached DUCHY BRENY. Refilled at VEZ. Proceeded with convoy to new Railhead at CREPY EN VALOIS	
8th October 1914. (CREPY)	Sent convoy under S.Sgt SHELTON to refill at BETHISY St PIERRE. (owing to fever or temporary rest list).	
9th October 1914. Travelling all night.	Filled at CREPY with 1 days supplies, proceeded en route for BELLEVILLE	Returned lorry 3 tons bag
10th October 1914. MONTREUIL	Reached BELLEVILLE at 2 p.m. had orders to proceed to ST OMER. ~~Started from~~ Reached MONTREUIL where we bivouacked for the night.	

Army Form C. 2118.

WAR DIARY
or
INTELLIGENCE SUMMARY.
(Erase heading not required.)

Instructions regarding War Diaries and Intelligence Summaries are contained in F.S. Regs., Part II. and the Staff Manual respectively. Title pages will be prepared in manuscript.

Hour, Date, Place	Summary of Events and Information	Remarks and references to Appendices
11th October 1914. ST OMER.	Reached ST OMER about noon.	Refilled (Train) attached to 1st Div. at ARQUES.
12th October 1914. LUMBRES	Collected after billets & report of 1st Div and then proceeded to railhead at LUMBRES wherein till 6.30. Received permission from Major Fasano to carry on to Belleby's area. Proceeded towards area at 10 pm.	"
13 October 1914 HAZEBROUCK.	Reached repelling point " at 5.30 am. Had to refill at BORRE. Collected ack ack at LE CINQ RUE & then returned to LUMBRES for men/rap supplies & returned to same repelling point at BORRE. Added to Bivouac at HAZEBRUCK.	Had to Refill at BORRE.
14 October 1914. THIENNES.	Reached THIENNES. Proceed to refill & joined at ROUGE CROIX & found Brigade had moved. Finally refilled at BAILLEUL.	Workshop & stonetruck to arise recouled.
15th October 1914. THIENNES	Reached THIENNES. Refilled at BAILLEUL	2nd Lt J.E. TAYLOR reports to duty.

(9.25.6) W 257—976 100,000 4/12 H W V   79/3298

WAR DIARY
INTELLIGENCE SUMMARY.
(Erase heading not required.)

Army Form C. 2118.

Hour, Date, Place	Summary of Events and Information	Remarks and references to Appendices
16th October 1914. VLAMERTINGHE.	Reached THIENNES. Refilled at VLAMERTINGHE, after having been ordered to proceed to NEUVE EGLISE.	
17th October 1914. VLAMERTINGHE	Returned to now Railhead ARNEKE. Refilled at VLAMERTINGHE. Now railhead at CAESTRE.	
18th October 1914. CAESTRE.	Reloaded at ARNEKE instead of CAESTRE. Refilled at VLAMERTINGHE.	
19th October 1914. CAESTRE	Reloaded at CAESTRE. Refilled at INN near STEENWERCK.	
20th October 1914. MERVILLE	Reloaded at MERVILLE. Refilled at LAVENTIE.	
21st October 1914. MERVILLE.	Reached MERVILLE. Refilled at crossroads North of SAILLY sur LYS.	
22nd October 1914.	Proceeded with extreme care to CROIX BLANCHE, reported to Brig: 14th Brigade under fire but to whom ordnance stores to pentilioespoint on supplies. Refilled at crossroads N of SAILLY.	

Army Form C. 2118.

WAR DIARY
or
INTELLIGENCE SUMMARY.
(Erase heading not required.)

Instructions regarding War Diaries and Intelligence Summaries are contained in F.S. Regs., Part II. and the Staff Manual respectively. Title pages will be prepared in manuscript.

Hour, Date, Place	Summary of Events and Information	Remarks and references to Appendices
23rd October 1914. MERVILLE	Railhead MERVILLE. Refilled at Nr SAILLY.	carried one advance
24th October 1914.	Railhead at St VENANT.	carried advance
to 31st October 1914 inclusive	Refilled Train at CROSSROADS North of SAILLY SUR LYS.	Store when relieving for 30th Signally sec

Ang 5/6

121/2649

19th Bde: Supply Column

Vol III. 1 – 30.11.14

WAR DIARY of XIXth Bde (Inf.) Supply Column

or INTELLIGENCE SUMMARY.

Army Form C.2118.

Instructions regarding War Diaries and Intelligence Summaries are contained in F.S. Regs., Part II. and the Staff Manual respectively. Title pages will be prepared in manuscript.

Hour, Date, Place	Summary of Events and Information	Remarks and references to Appendices
NOVEMBER 1914. 1st to 14th	Railhead ST VENANT. Refilling SAILLY sur LYS, Cross Roads North of —	
15th	Railhead ST VENANT. Refilling Point SAILLY sur LYS, CROSS ROADS North of.	First issue of butter in lieu of rations Bacon
16th	Railhead BASSE BOULONGE near MERVILLE. Refilling Point. SAILLY sur LYS, CROSS ROADS North of —	
17th to 19th	Railhead MERVILLE. Refilling Point. Railway Crossing W. of PONT de NIEPPE	
20th to 22nd	Railhead BASSE BOULONGE. Refilling Point. Railway Crossing W. of PONT de NIEPPE	
23rd to 30th	Railhead STEENWERCK. Refilling Point Railway Crossing W. of PONT de NIEPPE	

J.M. Clerke Capt.
O.C. XIXth Inf.
Bde Supply Column

121/3944

19th Bde Supply Col

Vol V 1 — 31.12.14

WAR DIARY

INTELLIGENCE SUMMARY

of 1/1/1 Bn Supply Column

Army Form C. 2118.

Hour, Date, Place	Summary of Events and Information	Remarks and references to Appendices
30 December 1914. NIEPPE	Leyland again broke down very universal buffer couplings gives way. New one sent for. Temporary repair carried out with bolts, shafts, but found unserviceable. Dump put up to within 50 yds at Railhead point. Railway crossing near PONT de NIEPPE returned to Railhead (closed). 5050 rations issued (entrance & personal services were carried out). Mac Raleys at long WALDDICOFF had raced into depot (lorries but not in depots) unparalleled difficulty by the and of an empty lorry the men of the column on returning to NIEPPE lorries were wasted time.	
31st December NIEPPE	Year finishes with a yesterday uninterrupted rout and thereafter. The repetity from Railhead remains. The same Lieut. TAYLOR returns H/Leave, but suffering from fever seeds put on the sick list. Lorries in good order except Motor car Leyland which required new universal joint. 2 new pistons. Refilling point Railway Crossing on PONT A NIEPPE Railhead STEENWERCK.	ATM R H Clarke Lieut Col

1247 W 3299 200,000 (E) 8/14 J.R.C. & A. Forms/C.2118/13.

WAR DIARY of XXVB Supply Column

INTELLIGENCE SUMMARY

Army Form C. 2118.

Instructions regarding War Diaries and Intelligence Summaries are contained in F. S. Regs., Part II. and the Staff Manual respectively. Title pages will be prepared in manuscript.

(Erase heading not required.)

Hour, Date, Place	Summary of Events and Information	Remarks and references to Appendices
1914		
26th December 1914 NIEPPE	Light day, no ordnance but heavy post & wireless which however were very late. 9 O/R. Lorry from 1st Divnl. Supply Dumped at Refilling point. Rest of Convoy near PONT de NIEPPE at 4 am (or so) at STEENWERCK for Rations returned to NIEPPE. Lorries unloaded down early now.	HAH
27th December 1914 NIEPPE	Fitted 2 new pistons to the Soccer Leyland Lorry. Dumped 2 some refilling point & proceeded STEENWERCK & also for Rations & usual post. Ordnance nothing extraordinary. Supplies the same.	HAH
28th December 1914 NIEPPE	Leyland again and & the 1 unrepaired, but Pistons Nº 3 & 4 we were expected to go at any moment new pistons were fordued not in stock. (dumped) supplies at same refilling point. Put Leyland on Post unloaded returned to STEENWERCK for 5000 rations. Usual ordnance service. Nothing important	HAH
29th December NIEPPE	Dumped at refilling point & picked up HAH Rincer many officers & subalterns were not returned to STEENWERCK where there were lorries over to the Railhead Supply Officer. I have got one or two also the presents to be carried this day. Two of our pls. for 5000 rations returned to NIEPPE chained down	HAH

1247 W 3290 200,000 (E) 8/14 J.B.C. &A. Forms/C. 2118/11.

WAR DIARY

of XLI B. de Supply Column

INTELLIGENCE SUMMARY

Army Form C. 2118

Hour, Date, Place	Summary of Events and Information	Remarks and references to Appendices
1914		
23rd December NIEPPE	Large consignment of Ordnance & Postage Stores today all being expect 30 cwt lorry had asked on for their load to do double journeys. After refilling in the morning at Railway siding near PONT DE NIEPPE Divisional Trans. [?] the ordnance & postal services Ron [?] was carried out, the ordnance & postal services returned to load supplies at STEENWERCK for servation returned to NIEPPE. Route change to [?] rendezvous.	(signed)
24 December NIEPPE	Severe filling point at 9 am. (Loaded) with usual supplies. (5700) at rendezvous part (2 Loads) Plum pudding short had to await arrival from NIEPPE on receiving orders to collect 2700 whom applied from passing train & Div. Train arrangement made into to proceed, with Ballins [?] way to PLOEGSTREET Village to collect these whom, Completed at 11 p.m.	(signed)
25 December NIEPPE	After refilling proceeded at 9.45 STEENWERCK at once loaded W.R.N. Provisions Mary gifts 5039 returned to Brigade Battalion Area in ARMENTIÈRES, where these were distributed before 1 pm. Meanwhile postal present services were carried out. The column (Loaded) with supplies returned to billets at NIEPPE for X mas dinners at 3 p.m. Ready after.	(signed)

WAR DIARY

of XIX Bde Supply Column

INTELLIGENCE SUMMARY

(Erase heading not required.)

Army Form C. 2118.

Instructions regarding War Diaries and Intelligence Summaries are contained in F. S. Regs., Part II. and the Staff Manual respectively. Title pages will be prepared in manuscript.

Hour, Date, Place	Summary of Events and Information	Remarks and references to Appendices
1914		
19th December NIEPPE	Nothing unusual. This day loaded up supplies for 2nd Division, moved to Divisional dumps & met Dumping and Refilling Point Railway Convoy, near PONT ROUGE. NIEPPE returned to NIEPPE railhead at all STEENWERCK.	APA
20th December NIEPPE	Heavy Ordnance mills company having 2 lorry loads of lorries overdone having body & journey spent & spare piston heads & oil way, got put up for non-return overtops. New parts wired for.	APA
21st December NIEPPE	Lorries with Ordnance parts & presents proceeded & met to Refilling point after loading, returned to STEENWERCK for supplies loaded with 5100 rations. Column remained loaded all night in the park used. Proceed to refilling point this day.	APA
22nd December NIEPPE	New System commenced. Proceeded with full supply lorries to some Refilling Point & dumped returned to STEENWERCK for supplies 5100 rations. The Ordnance & fuel lorries proceeded to STEENWERCK early, for their loads 2 lorries from supply section were sent to carry the extra amount. Column then returned to NIEPPE where lorries were washed down etc. This system is great improvement to the Column as regards hours (being practically in at night) also of the best compared all night.	Lieut & 71 for procee on 10 days leave. APA APA

1247 W 3299 200,000 (E) 8/14 J.B.C. & A. Forms/C.2118/1.

WAR DIARY
INTELLIGENCE SUMMARY

Army Form C. 2118.

1st B. Sub. Supply Column

(Erase heading not required.)

Instructions regarding War Diaries and Intelligence Summaries are contained in F. S. Regs., Part II. and the Staff Manual respectively. Title pages will be prepared in manuscript.

Hour, Date, Place	Summary of Events and Information	Remarks and references to Appendices
1914		
14 December NIEPPE	Though everything came out for duty, even satisfactorily. Loaded up at STEENWERCK & proceeded to same refilling point. Nothing unusual received this day. Returned to NIEPPE.	A17
15 December NIEPPE	Usual routine. Railhead at STEENWERCK. Some refilling point loaded 5200 rations revel. Parts of ordnance waste to go thoroughly cleaned. Lighting appears too overtaxed. Capt. Clarke informed. Same.	A18
16 December NIEPPE	Nothing unusual occurred. Railhead refilling point remain the same. Every body performs necessary advice, going to Railhead. Carry (ration) loaded 5100 to 5100 men returned to NIEPPE.	A19
17 December NIEPPE	Proceeded to STEENWERCK for 5100 rations twenty feet 1 December sent carry sent [?] route (to avoid main road). The main roads at 4 a.m. to carry rations for the slipper the train is refilling met to be taken up because of Territorial Bath 5 Rifles. The unit. So now they recognised. Returned to NIEPPE, to Refles. Gratuity. built over beds for lorries again in Leg condition.	A20
18 December NIEPPE	New system of refilling time discussed. Decided in future approved of Q.M.G. to refill in the morning men so bed at night. Usual routine carried out. Small Lorry ? to be put onto workshops for general cleaning up & overhaul.	A21

1247 W 3299 200,000 (E) 8/14 J.B.C. & A. Forms/C. 2118/11.

WAR DIARY
or
INTELLIGENCE SUMMARY X/X² Bde Supply Col.

Army Form C. 2118.

(Erase heading not required.)

Instructions regarding War Diaries and Intelligence Summaries are contained in F. S. Regs., Part II. and the Staff Manual respectively. Title pages will be prepared in manuscript.

Hour, Date, Place	Summary of Events and Information	Remarks and references to Appendices
1914		
10th December NIEPPE	Leyland Lorry ready for duty. With full complement of lorries the work was completed in no time. Day ended at STEENWERCK for 5200 men, proceeded. Wheeling crossing near PONT DE NIEPPE grating in hills at NIEPPE. Roads still heavy.	(initials)
11th December NIEPPE	Thornycroft Lorry put into workshops, new tongue tube to be fitted. Engine taken down. Renault Ford overhaul to be made. At STEENWERCK loaded supplies for 5200 men. Dennis (Hay) had to town extra clothing for ordnance. Same Refilling Point. Returned to NIEPPE on completion of duty.	(initials)
12th December NIEPPE	Thornycroft Lorry still under repair. Fitted new front wheels & returned old ones to base. Loaded at STEENWERCK for 5200 men. 2 lorries made an extra journey on account of carrying charcoal.	(initials)
13th December NIEPPE	Thornycroft Lorry ready for duty. Loaded at STEENWERCK for 5200 rations. Thornycroft had to be returned to base, the footbrake adjusted. Dennis 9 at same refilling point. Returned to NIEPPE.	(initials)

Army Form C. 2118.

WAR DIARY
of XIX Infantry Bde Supply Column.

INTELLIGENCE SUMMARY.

(Erase heading not required.)

Instructions regarding War Diaries and Intelligence Summaries are contained in F.S. Regs., Part II. and the Staff Manual respectively. Title pages will be prepared in manuscript.

Hour, Date, Place 1914	Summary of Events and Information	Remarks and references to Appendices
5th December LA CRÈCHE	Cleaned down Lorries and proceeded to STEENWERCK and M Ordnance 2 Lorries and Supplies for 4750 men proceeded to Refilling Point & dumped. Reserve orders to vacated LA CRECHE which was requisned by 4th Division. Gave orders to two billets at NIEPPE under approved H.Q's (Number HQ Renders assistance to fire Transport to London Rifle Bde Wagon Coy. Ditched for all goods and tents 11 Tonner Dept.	Proceed with M.S. M. SHELTON + PICKNANNIED on occasion of His Majesty the King's visit to his Troops. ASE 5th
6th December NIEPPE	After the proceeding magazine to England Bullets found in NIEPPE Lorries parked on St Squere. Wraps whistles held at Church. Brass hats to be made for the wheels. Bull em roads. Capt 4) in the afternoon for 4750 men with ususal ordnance spart. Returned to NIEPPE.	ASE 6th
7th December NIEPPE	Saturday usual turnout. Lorries to have new gears fitted. Lorries cleaned down. Loads of STEENWERCK for 4750 men and two loads of Ordnance, one lorry had to return for groceries.	ASE 7th
8th December NIEPPE	Lorries well under repair. Proceeded to STEENWERCK for 5200 rations there not in till late & Lorries were washed down. Refilling at same place near PONT de NIEPPE. Returned to NIEPPE after handing over supplies.	ASE 8th
9th December NIEPPE	Lorries taken out on new slight adjustments of required & was referring to workshop. Train again arrives late. Loaded for 5000 men with astelsbeek ordnance. Proceeds carried this day. Returned to NIEPPE. After dumping at same Refilling Point Railway Crossing near PONT à NIEPPE.	ASE 9th

WAR DIARY
of XIX Brigade Supply Column.
INTELLIGENCE SUMMARY.

(Erase heading not required.)

Army Form C. 2118.

Hour, Date, Place	Summary of Events and Information	Remarks and references to Appendices
1st December 19/14 LA CRECHE	Moved from MERVILLE to LA CRECHE. Proceeded to Railhead at STEENWERCK. Took 2 loads of ordnance + supplies for 4600 men with usual Post. Refilling point at Railway Crossing near PONT A NIEPPE, where supplies etc were dumped. Owing to the Train not arriving before 12 noon day was not finished till 6pm. Roads very heavy.	AM
2nd LA CRECHE	Chanced down lorries and proceeded to STEENWERCK on the arrival of the Railway Train. Loaded Supplies for 4600 men. Post of advance. Refilling Point at Railway Crossing near PONT de NIEPPE. Roads very heavy + delayed occasioned by horse columns running on same road in opposite directions. Dumped Supplies returned to LA CRECHE.	AM
3rd LA CRECHE	Leyland 1½ ton lorry motor heads gave way & put in workshop for repair. Rest of system (nic) With the rest of the column supplies were taken to STEENWERCK for 4750 men post ordnance + present. Dent presents direct to Refilling point near PONT de NIEPPE returned for Hay. Same Refilling point as yesterday. Column returned to La CRECHE.	AM
4th LA CRECHE.	Leyland out of workshop. New gear arrived for this Leyland with 4 speeds. Proceeded to Station STEENWERCK and loaded supplies as yesterday. Same refilling point.	AM

121/4447

19th Brigade. Supply Col"

Vol VI 1 — 31.1.15

Army Form C. 2118

WAR DIARY
or
INTELLIGENCE SUMMARY

(Erase heading not required.)

Instructions regarding War Diaries and Intelligence Summaries are contained in F. S. Regs, Part II. and the Staff Manual respectively. Title pages will be prepared in manuscript.

Hour, Date, Place	Summary of Events and Information	Remarks and references to Appendices
January 1915. 1st NIEPPE.	Proceeded to refilling point at Railway Crossing near PONT DE NIEPPE returned to Railhead at STEENWERCK, loaded 5000 rations, Ordnance Stores and Parcels for the troops. Had Convoy back to head a double journey. Returned to Nieppe, Convoy washed down etc. Weather fine, roads heavy.	[initials]
2nd do	Proceeded to refilling point at Railway Crossing near PONT DE NIEPPE returned to Railhead and loaded 4500 Rations Ordnance Stores, Mails and Parcels. On returning to Nieppe the handing Lorry had ditches, little delay caused. Lorries washed down etc. Weather fine, roads heavy.	[initials]
3rd do	Proceeded to refilling point at Railway Crossing near PONT DE NIEPPE and dumped supplies. Returned to Railhead. Hail Lorry (Leyland) under repair at Head Quarters, piston heads blown out. Loaded 4,7500 Rations. Bread Lorry had trouble in Caughnal. Returned to Nieppe. Lorries washed down etc. Weather wet, roads bad. One Leyland 3 Ton lorry exchanged for 1 Commer 3 Ton from A.H.Q.	[initials]

WAR DIARY
or
INTELLIGENCE SUMMARY

(Erase heading not required.)

Army Form C. 2118.

Instructions regarding War Diaries and Intelligence Summaries are contained in F. S. Regs., Part II. and the Staff Manual respectively. Title pages will be prepared in manuscript.

Hour, Date, Place	Summary of Events and Information	Remarks and references to Appendices
January 1915. 4th. NIEPPE.	Proceeded to same refilling point and dumped supplies. Returned to Railhead and loaded 5000 Rations. Hail. Completed dismantled, awaiting parts from M.T. Base. Lorey Army had to wait two hrs. Returned to Railhead. Returned to Nieppe. Lorries loaded dumed. 2 Thornycroft 3 Ton Lorries exchanges for 2, 3 Ton Commer from G.H.Q.	
5th. do.	Proceeded to same refilling point and dumped supplies. Returned to Railhead and loaded 5000 Rations. Returned to Nieppe, considerable delay en route on account of H.T. lorries loaded down etc. Weather fine. Roads clean.	
6th do	Proceeded to same refilling point and dumped supplies. Returned to Railhead and loaded 5000 Rations. Head completed made repair. Cabtoyries double journey. Returned to Nieppe. Lorries nailed down etc. Bennie Cary under repair dun'g return front spring centre bolt sheared. Weather wet, roads heavy.	

1247 W 3299 200,000 (E) 8/14 J.B.C. & A. Forms/C. 2118/11.

WAR DIARY
or
INTELLIGENCE SUMMARY

(Erase heading not required.)

Army Form C. 2118.

Hour, Date, Place	Summary of Events and Information	Remarks and references to Appendices
January 1915. 7th NIEPPE	Proceeded to same refilling point and dumped supplies. Returned to Railhead and loaded 5000 Rations. Lorries Completes made again Railway line to be double journey. Returned to Nieppe. Lorries waited down 15. Daimler lorry exchanged for 1 3 Ton Crossley from 2 Carlisle Column. The vehicle absolutely useless. eaten @ H.Q. trielaw.	JM
8th do	Proceeded to same refilling point and dumped the supplies. Returned to Railhead and loaded 5000 rations. Made light repairs. Returned to Nieppe. Advance slow, present train. Returned to Nieppe. Headlamp Autolegs, little delay. Lorrie waded down etc. weather fine, roads heavy.	JM
9th do	Proceeded to same refilling point and dumped supplies. Returned to Railhead and loaded 5300 Rations. Lorry (Napier) again made repair, pistons headgone. Returned to Nieppe, Lorries waded down etc. Weather wet, roads heavy.	JM
10th do	Proceeded to same refilling point and dumped supplies. Returned to Railhead and loaded 5300 rations. Lorries waded down etc. Also the Crossley obtained from the 2 Carl. Col. Lorry Conv. did double journey. Returned to Nieppe. Waded down Lorries etc. Weather wet. Roads heavy.	JM

Army Form C. 2118.

WAR DIARY
or
INTELLIGENCE SUMMARY

(Erase heading not required.)

Instructions regarding War Diaries and Intelligence Summaries are contained in F. S. Regs., Part II. and the Staff Manual respectively. Title pages will be prepared in manuscript.

Hour, Date, Place	Summary of Events and Information	Remarks and references to Appendices
January 1915. 11th, NIEPPE.	Proceeded to same refilling point and dumped supplies. Returned to Railhead at Steenwerck, loaded 5100 Rations. Bread lorry had to make double journey, had snowed. Convoy still under repair. Returned to Nieppe, loaded down. Convoy etc. weather fine, roads heavy.	
12th do	Proceeded to refilling point and dumped supplies. Returned to Railhead and loaded 5100 Rations. Uneventful day. Returned to Nieppe, Convoy locked down etc. Weather fine.	
13th do	Proceeded to same refilling point and dumped supplies. Returned to Railhead and loaded Rations. Went out during Subaltern late. Returned to Nieppe. Convoy lockdown etc. weather fine, roads heavy.	
14th do	Proceeded to same refilling point and dumped supplies. Returned to Railhead and loaded Rations. Lorry had to make double journey, delay caused on road on account of magneto trouble. Returned to Nieppe. Handed two lorry magnetos to workshop for adjusting. Convoy lockdown etc. Weather fine, roads slightly better.	

1217 W 3299 200,000 (E) 8/14 J.B.C. & A. Forms/C. 2118/11.

Army Form C. 2118.

WAR DIARY
— or —
INTELLIGENCE SUMMARY
(Erase heading not required.)

Instructions regarding War Diaries and Intelligence
Summaries are contained in F. S. Regs., Part II.
and the Staff Manual respectively. Title pages
will be prepared in manuscript.

Hour, Date, Place	Summary of Events and Information	Remarks and references to Appendices
January 1915. 15th. NIEPPE.	Proceeded to same refilling point and dumped supplies. Returned to Railhead and loaded Rations. Railhead wagon. Jenny lorry had to do double journey. Returned to trucks, lorries nailed down etc. Weather wet, roads heavy.	(Sd)
16th. do	Proceeded to same refilling point and dumped supplies. Returned to Railhead and loaded Rations. Hail and Comma Lorries still under repair. On returning Thorpe got Ammunition Choked but caused little delay. Lorries nailed down etc. Weather wet, roads heavy.	(Sd)
17th. do	Proceeded to same refilling point and dumped supplies. Lorries very difficult, considerable delay along convoy way nearly loaded. Returned to Railhead and loaded. Lorries nailed down etc. Hail and Comma Lorries still under repair. Weather wet, roads heavy.	(Sd)
18th. do	Proceeded to same refilling point and dumped supplies. Lorries and Hail lorries still under repair. Returned to Railhead and loaded Rations. Column renewed loaded all night as usual. Weather fine, roads heavy.	(Sd)

1247 W 3299 200,000 (E) 8/14 J.B.C. & A. Forms/C.2118/11.

Army Form C. 2118.

WAR DIARY
or
INTELLIGENCE SUMMARY

(Erase heading not required.)

Instructions regarding War Diaries and Intelligence Summaries are contained in F.S. Regs., Part II. and the Staff Manual respectively. Title pages will be prepared in manuscript.

Hour, Date, Place	Summary of Events and Information	Remarks and references to Appendices
January 1915. 19th NIEPPE.	Proceeded to same refilling point and dumped supplies, had one horse cast in de chair. Returned to Renescure and loaded Rations. Uneventful return journey to troops. Horses washed down etc. Weather wet, roads heavy.	
20th do	Proceeded to same refilling point and dumped supplies, had one horse cast in de chair. Returned to Renescure and loaded Rations. Supply train late. Present and others stood by. Returned to the HQ considerably delayed owing to traffic on narrow road. Horses washed down etc. Weather fine, roads heavy.	
21st do	Proceeded to same refilling point and dumped supplies, had any horses and returned to Renescure and loaded Rations. Returned to troops. Weather wet, roads heavy.	
22nd do	Proceeded to new refilling point at RUE DES ACQUETS near ARMENTIERRE dumped supplies and returned to Renescure. One horse cast in repair and returned to troops. had row again in de repair. Loaded Rations and returned to troops. Horses washed down etc. Weather fine, roads heavy.	

WAR DIARY
or
INTELLIGENCE SUMMARY

(Erase heading not required.)

Army Form C. 2118.

Hour, Date, Place	Summary of Events and Information	Remarks and references to Appendices
January 9.5.23rd NIEPPE.	Proceeded to same refilling point and dumped supplies. Returned to Railhead and loaded. Returns. Mail lorry under repair. Returned to Nieppe. Lorries unloaded down etc. Weather fine. Whilst in proceeded on leave to England.	
24th do	Proceeded to same refilling point and dumped supplies. Returned to Railhead and loaded Returns. Had very wet day. Brewery lorry had to make two journeys. Returned to Nieppe and unloaded. Lorries down. Weather wet. Roadclean	
25th do	Proceeded to same refilling point and dumped supplies. Mail lorry still under repair. Proceeded to Railhead and loaded Returns. Grocery lorry had to make a double journey. Returned to Nieppe. Lorries unloaded etc. Weather wet. Roadclean.	
26th do	Proceeded to same refilling point and dumped supplies. Mail lorry still under repair. Returned to Railhead and loaded Returns. Thereafter return journey to Nieppe. Weather fine. Lorries unloaded down etc. Roadclean.	

Army Form C. 2118.

WAR DIARY
or
INTELLIGENCE SUMMARY
(Erase heading not required.)

Instructions regarding War Diaries and Intelligence Summaries are contained in F. S. Regs., Part II. and the Staff Manual respectively. Title pages will be prepared in manuscript.

Hour, Date, Place	Summary of Events and Information	Remarks and references to Appendices
January 1915. 27th - NIEPPE	Proceeded to same refilling point and dumped supplies. Mail completed under repair. Returned to Railhead and loaded Rations. Advanced Store heavy, cart horses tired to make a double journey. Returned to Nieppe, horses walked down ells. head fire, was bad.	[signature]
28th do	Proceeded to same refilling point and dumped supplies. Still under repair. Returned to Railhead and loaded Rations. Cart horses tired to make a second journey. Returned and ells Horses walked down ells. heath fine. Roads slight.	[signature]
29th do	Proceeded to same refilling point and dumped supplies. Mail lorry still under repair. Returned to Railhead unloaded Rations. Returned to Nieppe. Commenced down ells. Nearly fine, roads bad.	[signature]
30th do	Proceeded to same refilling point and dumped supplies. Mail lorry still under repair. Returned to Railhead and loaded Rations. Shells dropped within the vicinity of Railhead. Returned to Nieppe and walked horses down. Weather wet. In full action returned from leave.	[signature]

1247 W 3299 200,000 (E) 8/14 J.B.C. & A.   Forms/C. 2118/11.

Army Form C. 2118.

WAR DIARY
or
INTELLIGENCE SUMMARY
(Erase heading not required.)

Instructions regarding War Diaries and Intelligence Summaries are contained in F. S. Regs., Part II. and the Staff Manual respectively. Title pages will be prepared in manuscript.

Hour, Date, Place	Summary of Events and Information	Remarks and references to Appendices
January 1915. 31st. MEPPE	Proceeded to some refilling point and dumped outfits. New Railhead today at STRAZEELE, issued Rations and returned to depot at 6 p.m. Weather wet. Roads heavy.	[signature]

H.M. Carter Major.
O.C. XIX Div Supply Column.

121/5255

19th Brigade Supply: Colu.

Vols: VII, VIII & IX   6.2. — 30.4.15

WAR DIARY
INTELLIGENCE SUMMARY
(Erase heading not required.)

Army Form C. 2118.

February 1915.

19th Inf Bde Supply Column.

WAR DIARY of XIXth Infantry Brigade Army Form C. 2118.
Supply Column.

or

INTELLIGENCE SUMMARY

(Erase heading not required.)

Instructions regarding War Diaries and Intelligence
Summaries are contained in F. S. Regs., Part II.
and the Staff Manual respectively. Title pages
will be prepared in manuscript.

Hour, Date, Place	Summary of Events and Information	Remarks and references to Appendices
6th February, 1915. Nieppe.	Took over XIXth Infantry Brigade Supply Column. Proceeded to refilling point near Pont de Nieppe. Returned to railhead. (STEENWERK) and refilled. No train arrived so refilled from surplus from 3rd Army Corps Supply train and from reserve rations at railhead.	A.9.1 ⇒
7th Feb. 1915. --- Nieppe.	Proceeded to refilling point near Pont de Nieppe. Returned to railhead (STEENWERK) and refilled. 1 Commer Lorry (3 Ton) received from 8th Div. Supply Column, 1 Leyland Lorry handed over in exchange.	A.9.1 ⇒
8th Feb 1915. --- Nieppe.	Proceeded to refilling point near Pont de Nieppe. Returned to railhead & refilled.	A.9.1 ⇒
9th Feb 1915. --- Nieppe.	Proceeded to refilling point near Pont de Nieppe. Returned to railhead and refilled. Overdue tobacco ration arrived	A.9.1 ⇒

WAR DIARY

of XIXth Infantry Brigade Supply Column.

INTELLIGENCE SUMMARY

Army Form C. 2118.

(Erase heading not required.)

Instructions regarding War Diaries and Intelligence Summaries are contained in F. S. Regs., Part II. and the Staff Manual respectively. Title pages will be prepared in manuscript.

Hour, Date, Place	Summary of Events and Information	Remarks and references to Appendices
10th Feb.1915. --- Nieppe.	Proceeded to refilling point near PONT de NIEPPE. Returned to railhead (STEENWERK) and refilled. Pte Daniells went sick.	A.9.1.D
11th Feb.1915. --- Nieppe.	Proceeded to refilling point near PONT de NIEPPE. Returned to railhead (STEENWERK) and refilled. 1 Conner Lorry went to ISBERGUES to be retyred.	A.9.1.D
12th Feb.1915. --- Nieppe.	Proceeded to refilling point near PONT de NIEPPE. Returned to railhead (STEENWERK) and refilled. Maudeslay lorry broke 1 front axel / rear spring, the latter being formerly in a bad state.	A.9.1.D
13th Feb.1915. --- Nieppe.	Proceeded to refilling point near PONT de NIEPPE. Returned to railhead (STEENWERK) and refilled. Motor cyclist took returns to Q.H.Qrs, no car being available.	A.9.1.D
14th Feb.1915. --- Nieppe.	Proceeded to refilling point near PONT de NIEPPE. Returned to railhead (STEENWERK) and refilled	A.9.1.D

WAR DIARY
of 19th Infantry Brigade Supply Column
INTELLIGENCE SUMMARY

Army Form C. 2118.

(Erase heading not required.)

Hour, Date, Place	Summary of Events and Information	Remarks and references to Appendices
15th Feb. 1915. — Nieppe.	Proceeded to refilling point near Pont de Nieppe. Returned to railhead (STEENWERK) and refilled. The 5 Ton Commer lorry went to ISEBERGUES to be retyred.	A.9.1.
16th Feb. 1915. — Nieppe.	Proceeded to refilling point near Pont de Nieppe. Returned to railhead (STEENWERK) and refilled.	A.9.1.
17th Feb. 1915. — Nieppe.	Proceeded to refilling point near Pont de Nieppe. Returned to railhead (STEENWERK) and refilled. Pte Lewis of the Middlesex Regt. joined for a lorry driving test.	A.9.1.
18th Feb. 1915. — Nieppe.	Proceeded to refilling point near Pont de Nieppe. Returned to railhead (STEENWERK) and refilled. 2,300 grocery rations came up on the train.	A.9.1.

WAR DIARY
of X/XI Infantry Brigade Supply Column.
INTELLIGENCE SUMMARY

Army Form C. 2118.

(Erase heading not required.)

Instructions regarding War Diaries and Intelligence Summaries are contained in F. S. Regs., Part II. and the Staff Manual respectively. Title pages will be prepared in manuscript.

Hour, Date, Place	Summary of Events and Information	Remarks and references to Appendices
19 Feb. 1915 - - - Nieppe.	Proceeded to refilling point near Pont de Nieppe. Returned to railhead (STEENWERK) and refilled.	X.9.1.D
20 Feb 1915 - - - Nieppe.	Proceeded to refilling point near Pont de Nieppe. Returned to railhead (STEENWERK) and refilled. Motor car M.642 despatched to GENNEVILLIERS.	X.9.1.D
21st Feb 1915 - - - Nieppe.	Proceeded to refilling point near Pont de Nieppe. Returned to railhead (STEENWERK) and refilled. Lorry proceeded to X/IX Infantry Brigade HQrs to take Officers on leave.	X.9.1.D
22nd Feb 1915 - - - Nieppe.	Proceeded to refilling point near Pont de Nieppe. Returned to railhead (STEENWERK) and refilled. Dennis lorry damaged its differential gear.	X.9.1.D

Army Form C. 2118.

WAR DIARY

of 2×1×5 Infantry Brigade Supply Column

INTELLIGENCE SUMMARY

(Erase heading not required.)

Instructions regarding War Diaries and Intelligence
Summaries are contained in F. S. Regs., Part II.
and the Staff Manual respectively. Title pages
will be prepared in manuscript.

Hour, Date, Place	Summary of Events and Information	Remarks and references to Appendices
23rd Feb 1915 - Nieppe.	Proceeded to refilling point near PONT de NIEPPE. Returned to railhead (STEENWERK) and refilled.	A.9.1. ⊃
24th Feb 1915 - Nieppe.	Proceeded to refilling point near PONT de NIEPPE. Returned to railhead (STEENWERK) and refilled. Supply train did not arrive until 11.40 am.	A.9.1. ⊃
25th Feb 1915 - Nieppe.	Proceeded to refilling point near PONT de NIEPPE. Returned to railhead (STEENWERK) and refilled. Daimler motor car fetched from HAZEBROUCK for the Column.	A.9.1. ⊃
26th Feb 1915 - Nieppe.	Proceeded to refilling point near PONT de NIEPPE. Returned to railhead (STEENWERK) and refilled.	A.9.1. ⊃

WAR DIARY

of XIX 2 Infantry Brigade Supply Column

INTELLIGENCE SUMMARY

Army Form C. 2118.

(Erase heading not required.)

Instructions regarding War Diaries and Intelligence Summaries are contained in F. S. Regs., Part II. and the Staff Manual respectively. Title pages will be prepared in manuscript.

Hour, Date, Place	Summary of Events and Information	Remarks and references to Appendices
27th Feb 1915. — Nieppe.	Proceeded to refilling point near Pont de Nieppe. Returned to railhead (STEENWERK) and refilled. Weekly returns taken to DD of S+T. (HAZEBROUCK)	Jt.9.1.D
28th Feb 1915. — Nieppe.	Proceeded to refilling point near Pont de Nieppe. Returned to railhead (STEENWERK) and refilled. Supply train did not arrive until about 11 a.m.	Jt.9.1.D

Army Form C. 2118.

WAR DIARY
INTELLIGENCE SUMMARY
(Erase heading not required.)

March 1915.

19 R. Inf. Bde Supply Column.

Army Form C. 2118.

WAR DIARY
~~or~~ INTELLIGENCE SUMMARY 19th Inf. Bde. Supply Col
(Erase heading not required.)

Instructions regarding War Diaries and Intelligence Summaries are contained in F. S. Regs., Part II. and the Staff Manual respectively. Title pages will be prepared in manuscript.

Hour, Date, Place	Summary of Events and Information	Remarks and references to Appendices
1st March 1915 — Nieppe.	Proceeded to refilling point near Pont de Nieppe, dumped and returned to railhead (STEENWERK) and refilled. No bread and grocery truck arrived, so deficiency was made up from the 5th Seaforth haul and also from BAILLEUL	A.9.1.D
2nd March 1915 — Nieppe.	Proceeded to refilling point near Pont de Nieppe, dumped and returned to railhead (STEENWERK). Commer long chassis No. 1230 broke down.	A.9.1.D
3rd March 1915 — Nieppe.	Proceeded to refilling point near Pont de Nieppe, dumped and returned to railhead (STEENWERK). Sent Dennis lorry 3 ton chassis no 661, to ROUEN.	A.9.1.D
4th March 1915 — Nieppe.	Proceeded to refilling point near Pont de Nieppe, dumped and returned to railhead (STEENWERK) and refilled.	A.9.1.D

Army Form C. 2118.

WAR DIARY
of
INTELLIGENCE SUMMARY 19th My. Bde. Supply Col.
(Erase heading not required.)

Instructions regarding War Diaries and Intelligence Summaries are contained in F. S. Regs., Part II. and the Staff Manual respectively. Title pages will be prepared in manuscript.

Hour, Date, Place	Summary of Events and Information	Remarks and references to Appendices
5th March 1915 — Nieppe	Proceeded to refilling point near Pont de Nieppe, dumped and returned to railhead (STEENWERK) and refilled.	A.9.1.D
6th March 1915 — Nieppe	Proceeded to refilling point near Pont de Nieppe, dumped and returned to railhead (STEENWERK) and refilled. 10th Section train came up with 5,700 rations. Lieut Tylor admitted to hospital.	A.9.1.D
7th March 1915 — Nieppe	Proceeded to refilling point near Pont de Nieppe, dumped (STEENWERK) and returned to railhead and refilled.	A.9.1.D
8th March 1915 — Nieppe	Proceeded to refilling point near Pont de Nieppe, dumped and returned to railhead (STEENWERK) and refilled.	A.9.9.D
9th March 1915 — Nieppe	Proceeded to refilling point near Pont de Nieppe, dumped and returned to railhead (STEENWERK) and refilled. Commer lorry Chassis No 1280 despatched to GENNEVILLIERS	A.9.1.D

Army Form C. 2118.

WAR DIARY
INTELLIGENCE SUMMARY 19th Inf. Bde. Supply Col.

(Erase heading not required.)

Instructions regarding War Diaries and Intelligence Summaries are contained in F. S. Regs., Part II. and the Staff Manual respectively. Title pages will be prepared in manuscript.

Hour, Date, Place	Summary of Events and Information	Remarks and references to Appendices
10th March 1915 --- Nieppe.	Proceeded to refilling point near Pont de Nieppe, dumped and returned to railhead (STEENWERK) and refilled.	A.9.1.C.
11th March 1915 --- Nieppe.	Proceeded to refilling point near Pont de Nieppe, dumped and returned to railhead (STEENWERK) and refilled.	A.9.1.C.
12th March 1915 --- Nieppe.	Proceeded to refilling point near Pont de Nieppe, dumped and returned to railhead (STEENWERK) and refilled.	A.9.1.C.
13th March 1915 --- Nieppe.	Proceeded to refilling point near Pont de Nieppe, dumped and returned to railhead (STEENWERK) and refilled.	A.9.1.C.
14th March 1915 --- Nieppe.	Proceeded to refilling point near Pont de Nieppe, dumped and returned to railhead (STEENWERK) and refilled. In the morning I visited the D.D. of S.+T. 2nd Army, re lorries	A.9.1.C.

Army Form C. 2118.

WAR DIARY
of
INTELLIGENCE SUMMARY 19th Iny. Bde. Supply Col.

(Erase heading not required.)

Instructions regarding War Diaries and Intelligence Summaries are contained in F. S. Regs., Part II. and the Staff Manual respectively. Title pages will be prepared in manuscript.

Hour, Date, Place	Summary of Events and Information	Remarks and references to Appendices
15th March 1915 — Nieppe.	Proceeded to refilling point near Pont de Nieppe, dumped and returned to railhead (STEENWERK) and refilled. Napier lorry sent to ISBERGUES to have rear wheel refixed. The lorry returned in the evening.	14.9.1.⊃
16th March 1915 — Nieppe.	Proceeded to refilling point near Pont de Nieppe, dumped and returned to railhead (STEENWERK) and refilled.	14.9.1.⊃
17th March 1915 — Nieppe.	Proceeded to refilling point near Pont de Nieppe, dumped and returned to railhead (STEENWERK) and refilled. Proceeded to DD of S + T 2nd Army and fetched 1.8 Ton and 1 30cwt lorries.	14.9.1.⊃
18th March 1915 — Nieppe.	Proceeded to the refilling point near Pont de Nieppe, dumped and returned to railhead (STEENWERK) and refilled. Tested 'Weed' non-skids.	14.9.1.⊃

1247 W 3299 200,000 (E) 8/14 J.B.C. & A. Forms/C. 2118/11.

Army Form C. 2118.

WAR DIARY
INTELLIGENCE SUMMARY (Q.F. 3rd Poole Supply Col.)

(Erase heading not required.)

Instructions regarding War Diaries and Intelligence Summaries are contained in F. S. Regs., Part II. and the Staff Manual respectively. Title pages will be prepared in manuscript.

Hour, Date, Place	Summary of Events and Information	Remarks and references to Appendices
19th March 1915 — Mieppe.	Proceeded to refilling point near Pont de Mieppe, dumped and returned to railhead (STEENWERK) and refilled. 1 Comm. lorry went to ISEBERGUES to be returned.	A.9.1.5
20th March 1915 — Mieppe.	Proceeded to refilling point near Pont de Mieppe, dumped and returned to railhead (STEENWERK) and refilled.	A.9.1.5
21st March 1915 — Mieppe.	Proceeded to refilling point near Pont de Mieppe, dumped and returned to railhead (STEENWERK) and refilled.	A.9.1.5
22nd March 1915 —	Changed refilling point to cross roads near railway crossing near Pont de Mieppe dumped and returned to railhead (STEENWERK) and refilled. the Red Commer broke down.	A.9.1.5

Army Form C. 2118.

WAR DIARY
of
INTELLIGENCE SUMMARY 19th Inf. Bde. Supply Col.
(Erase heading not required.)

Instructions regarding War Diaries and Intelligence Summaries are contained in F. S. Regs., Part II. and the Staff Manual respectively. Title pages will be prepared in manuscript.

Hour, Date, Place	Summary of Events and Information	Remarks and references to Appendices
23rd March 1915 --- Nieppe.	Proceeded to refilling point at cross roads near railway crossing near PONT de Nieppe, dumped and returned to railhead (STEENWERK) and refilled.	A.F.C.9.
24th March 1915 --- Nieppe.	Proceeded to refilling point at cross roads near railway crossing near PONT de Nieppe, dumped and returned to railhead (STEENWERK) and refilled. 2nd Lt. Tylor admitted to hospital.	A.F.C.9.
25th March 1915 --- Nieppe.	Proceeded to refilling point at cross roads near railway crossing near PONT de Nieppe, dumped and returned to railhead (STEENWERK) and refilled	A.F.C.9.
26th March 1915 --- Nieppe.	Proceeded to refilling point at cross roads near railway crossing near PONT de Nieppe, dumped and returned to railhead (STEENWERK) and refilled. Common no 187 broke down.	A.F.C.9.

Army Form C. 2118.

WAR DIARY
~~or~~ INTELLIGENCE SUMMARY 19th Inf. Bde. Supply Col.

(Erase heading not required.)

Instructions regarding War Diaries and Intelligence Summaries are contained in F.S. Regs., Part II. and the Staff Manual respectively. Title pages will be prepared in manuscript.

Hour, Date, Place	Summary of Events and Information	Remarks and references to Appendices
27th March 1915 – Nieppe.	Proceeded to refilling point at cross roads near railway crossing near Pont de Nieppe, dumped and returned to railhead (STEENWERK) and refilled. Commen wo 187 also Pt SMART sent to GENNEVILLIERS.	A.F.91.7
28th March 1915 – Nieppe.	Proceeded to refilling point at cross roads near railway crossing near Pont de Nieppe; dumped and returned to railhead (STEENWERK) and refilled.	A.F.91.7
29th March 1915 – Nieppe.	Proceeded to refilling point at cross roads near railway crossing near Pont de Nieppe, dumped and returned to railhead (STEENWERK) and refilled. Mandeslauf lorry proceeded to refining plant ISBERGUES.	A.F.91.7

Army Form C. 2118.

WAR DIARY
of
INTELLIGENCE SUMMARY 19th - 2nd of Bde Supply Col.
(Erase heading not required.)

Hour, Date, Place	Summary of Events and Information	Remarks and references to Appendices
30th March 1915 --- Nieppe	Proceeded to refilling point at crossroads near railway crossing near PONT de Nieppe, dumped and returned to railhead and refilled.	
31st March 1915 --- Nieppe.	Proceeded to refilling point at cross roads near railway crossing near Pont de Nieppe, dumped and returned to railhead and refilled. Received one 3 Ton Commer from 3rd Divi. Supply Column	

Army Form C. 2118.

WAR DIARY
INTELLIGENCE SUMMARY
(Erase heading not required.)

Instructions regarding War Diaries and Intelligence Summaries are contained in F. S. Regs., Part II. and the Staff Manual respectively. Title pages will be prepared in manuscript.

Hour, Date, Place	Summary of Events and Information	Remarks and references to Appendices
	April. 1915. 19th Dy Bde Supply Column.	

Army Form C. 2118.

WAR DIARY
of
INTELLIGENCE SUMMARY

19th Inf. Bde. Supply Column

(Erase heading not required.)

Instructions regarding War Diaries and Intelligence Summaries are contained in F. S. Regs., Part II. and the Staff Manual respectively. Title pages will be prepared in manuscript.

Hour, Date, Place	Summary of Events and Information	Remarks and references to Appendices
1st April 1915 — Nieppe.	Proceeded to refilling point at cross roads near railway crossing near Pont de Nieppe, dumped and returned to railhead (STEENWERK) and refilled. Received one 3 Ton Commer lorry from 3rd Div. Supply Column.	A.9.1.D
2nd April 1915 — Nieppe.	Proceeded to refilling point at cross roads near railway crossing near Pont de Nieppe, dumped and returned to railhead (STEENWERK) and refilled. Handed over one 3 Ton Mercedes lorry to 28th Div. Supply Col.	A.9.1.D
3rd April 1915 — Nieppe.	Proceeded to refilling point at cross roads near railway crossing near Pont de Nieppe, dumped and returned to railhead (STEENWERK) and refilled. Pte Holm admitted to hospital.	A.9.1.D
4th April 1915 — Nieppe.	Proceeded to refilling point at cross roads near railway crossing near Pont de Nieppe, dumped and returned to railhead (STEENWERK) and refilled.	A.9.1.D

Army Form C. 2118.

WAR DIARY
of
INTELLIGENCE SUMMARY 19th Inf Bde Supply Column

(Erase heading not required.)

Instructions regarding War Diaries and Intelligence Summaries are contained in F. S. Regs., Part II. and the Staff Manual respectively. Title pages will be prepared in manuscript.

Hour, Date, Place	Summary of Events and Information	Remarks and references to Appendices
5th April 1915 — Nieppe.	Proceeded to refilling point at cross roads near railway crossing near Pont de Nieppe; dumped and returned to railhead (STEENWERK) and refilled.	A.S.I.D
6th April 1915 — Nieppe.	Proceeded to refilling point at cross roads near railway crossing near Pont de Nieppe; dumped and returned to railhead (STEENWERK) and refilled. One lorry on duty carrying coke for the 19th Inf Bde.	A.S.I.D
7th April 1915 — Nieppe	Proceeded to refilling point at cross roads near railway crossing near Pont de Nieppe; dumped and returned to railhead (STEENWERK) and refilled. Two lorries on duty carrying coke from STEENWERK Station in the afternoon. M.S.M. E.F. OSMAN transferred to 2nd Cav Div Supply Column.	A.S.I.D

WAR DIARY
of
INTELLIGENCE SUMMARY 19th Inf. Bde. Supply Column.

(Erase heading not required.)

Army Form C. 2118.

Hour, Date, Place	Summary of Events and Information	Remarks and references to Appendices
8. April 1915. -- Nieppe.	Proceeded to refilling point at cross roads near railway crossing near Pont de Nieppe, dumped and returned to railhead (STEENWERK) and refilled. Common Lorry No 4480 broke down. Dumped three lorry loads of supplies in the after noon so as to fetch straw from the station for the 19th Inf Bde Train.	No 9/1. D
9th April 1915 -- Nieppe.	Proceeded to refilling point at cross roads near railway crossing near Pont de Nieppe, dumped and returned to railhead (STEENWERK) and refilled.	No 9/1. D

WAR DIARY
or
INTELLIGENCE SUMMARY 19th Ind. Bde. Supply Column

Army Form C. 2118.

(Erase heading not required.)

Hour, Date, Place	Summary of Events and Information	Remarks and references to Appendices
10th April 1915 --- Nieppe.	Proceeded to refilling point at cross roads near railway crossing near Pont de Nieppe, dumped and returned to railhead (STEENWERK) and refilled. Train did return trip after 12 noon	17.9.15
11th April 1915 --- Nieppe.	Proceeded to refilling point at cross roads near railway crossing near Pont de Nieppe, dumped and returned to railhead (STEENWERK) and refilled. 3 Ton lorries sent to Glamorgan Fortress Coy. Demros " " Hdqrs. 2nd Corps. Cormier (3 Ton) returned from --- " " " --- Pack Artillery Park	17.9.15
12th April 1915 --- Nieppe.	Proceeded to refilling point at cross roads near railway crossing near Pont de Nieppe, dumped returned to railhead (STEENWERK) and refilled.	17.9.15

Army Form C. 2118.

WAR DIARY
or
INTELLIGENCE SUMMARY 19th Inf. Bde. Supply Column

(Erase heading not required.)

Instructions regarding War Diaries and Intelligence Summaries are contained in F. S. Regs, Part II. and the Staff Manual respectively. Title pages will be prepared in manuscript.

Hour, Date, Place	Summary of Events and Information	Remarks and references to Appendices
13th April 1915 --- Nieppe.	Proceeded to refilling point at cross roads near railway crossing near Pont de Nieppe, dumped and returned to railhead (STEENWERK) and refilled. 2nd Lt. J. Taylor returned to duty.	A.F.91.D
14th April 1915 --- Nieppe.	Proceeded to refilling point at crossroads near railway crossing near Pont de Nieppe, dumped and returned to railhead (STEENWERK) and refilled.	A.F.91.D
15th April 1915 --- Nieppe.	Proceeded to refilling point at cross roads near railway crossing near Pont de Nieppe, dumped and refilled. Four lorries on duty, carrying straw in the afternoon. Train did not arrive till 12.5 pm.	A.F.91.D

WAR DIARY
of
INTELLIGENCE SUMMARY 19th Base Supply Column.

Army Form C. 2118.

(Erase heading not required.)

Instructions regarding War Diaries and Intelligence Summaries are contained in F. S. Regs., Part II. and the Staff Manual respectively. Title pages will be prepared in manuscript.

Hour, Date, Place	Summary of Events and Information	Remarks and references to Appendices
16th April 1915 — Nieppe	Proceeded to refilling point at cross roads near railway crossing near Pont de Nieppe; dumped and returned to railhead (STEENWERK) and refilled. £10/5 Section train did not arrive until 1.15 p.m. One lorry carrying shaw in the morning.	A.S.J.S.D
17th April 1915 — Nieppe	Proceeded to refilling point at cross roads near railway crossing near Pont de Nieppe; dumped and returned to railhead (STEENWERK) and refilled. 11 Soldiers joined from BASE, also M.SS. SHEPPERD and W.SS. NEEDHAM from 2nd Anti Air Craft Workshop Unit	A.S.J.S.D
18th April 1915 — Nieppe	Proceeded to refilling point at cross roads near railway crossing near Pont de Nieppe; dumped and returned to railhead (STEENWERK) and refilled. Ptes Day and Wilcox despatched to ROUEN. (Surplus M.T. drivers).	A.S.J.S.D

Army Form C. 2118.

WAR DIARY
of
INTELLIGENCE SUMMARY 19th Ind. Bde. Supply Column.

(Erase heading not required.)

Instructions regarding War Diaries and Intelligence Summaries are contained in F. S. Regs., Part II. and the Staff Manual respectively. Title pages will be prepared in manuscript.

Hour, Date, Place	Summary of Events and Information	Remarks and references to Appendices
19th April 1915 --- Nieppe.	Proceeded to refilling point at cross roads near railway crossing near PONT de NIEPPE, dumped and returned to railhead (STEENWERK) and refilled. 2 S/Sgts from to ~~8th Queen's Royal Stafford Regt.~~ — 11 loaders and 3 fitters from BASE reported to this unit yesterday, for duty.	It. 91. C
20th April 1915 --- Nieppe.	Proceeded to refilling point at cross roads near railway crossing near PONT de NIEPPE, dumped and returned to railhead (STEENWERK) and refilled.	It. 91. C
21st April 1915 --- Nieppe.	Proceeded to refilling point at cross roads near railway crossing near PONT de NIEPPE, dumped and returned to railhead (STEENWERK) and refilled. 30 Cwt Commer No 6401 Sent to D.D. of S. ↱ T 1st Army	It. 91. C

Army Form C. 2118.

WAR DIARY

INTELLIGENCE SUMMARY 10th Infantry Brigade Supply Col.

(Erase heading not required.)

Instructions regarding War Diaries and Intelligence Summaries are contained in F. S. Regs., Part II. and the Staff Manual respectively. Title pages will be prepared in manuscript.

Hour, Date, Place	Summary of Events and Information	Remarks and references to Appendices
22nd April 1915 — Nieppe.	Proceeded to refilling point at cross roads near railway crossing near Pont de Nieppe, dumped and returned to railhead (STEENWERK) and refilled. Fetched a 30 cwt. Cowmen lorry from DD of S. T. 2nd Army.	17.9.15
23rd April 1915 — Nieppe	Proceeded to refilling point at cross roads near railway crossing near Pont de Nieppe, dumped and returned to railhead (STEENWERK) and refilled. Dumped 5 lorry loads of supplies at 2pm and returned to railhead; loaded up with Shaw and returned to Nieppe.	17.9.15
24th April 1915 — Nieppe.	Proceeded to refilling point at cross roads near railway crossing near Pont de Nieppe, dumped and returned to railhead (STEENWERK) and refilled.	17.9.15

Army Form C. 2118.

WAR DIARY
or
INTELLIGENCE SUMMARY
(Erase heading not required.)

Instructions regarding War Diaries and Intelligence Summaries are contained in F. S. Regs., Part II. and the Staff Manual respectively. Title pages will be prepared in manuscript.

Hour, Date, Place	Summary of Events and Information	Remarks and references to Appendices
25th April 1915 ---- Nieppe.	Proceeded to refilling point at cross roads near railway crossing near Pont de Nieppe, dumped and returned to railhead (STEENWERK) and refilled.	J.9.1.C
26th April 1915 ---- Nieppe.	Proceeded to refilling point at cross roads near railway crossing near Pont de Nieppe, dumped and returned to railhead (STEENWERK) and refilled. Dumped at 7.15 a.m.	J.9.1.C
27th April 1915 ---- Nieppe.	Proceeded to refilling point at cross roads near railway crossing near Pont de Nieppe, dumped and returned to railhead (STEENWERK) and refilled. Dumped at 7.15 a.m. Received 5 hours from 5th Divl Supply Col.	J.9.1.C

Army Form C. 2118.

WAR DIARY
or
INTELLIGENCE SUMMARY

192nd. Bde. Supply Col.

(Erase heading not required.)

Instructions regarding War Diaries and Intelligence Summaries are contained in F. S. Regs., Part II. and the Staff Manual respectively. Title pages will be prepared in manuscript.

Hour, Date, Place	Summary of Events and Information	Remarks and references to Appendices
28th April 1915 --- Nieppe.	Proceeded to refilling point at cross roads near railway crossing near Pont de Nieppe, dumped at 1.15am and returned to railhead (STEENWERK) and refilled. Dumped 4 lorry loads of Supplies at 2pm, returned to railhead and loaded up - 8½ tons 2 haws - 1 ton coke - 21 sacks of charcoal. Returned to Nieppe.	A.9.1.D
29th April 1915 --- Nieppe	Proceeded to refilling point at cross roads near railway crossing near Pont de Nieppe, dumped at 7.20 am and returned to railhead (STEENWERK) and refilled. Dumped. Returned to Nieppe.	A.9.1.D
30th April 1915 --- Nieppe.	Proceeded to refilling point at cross roads near railway crossing near Pont de Nieppe, dumped at 7.15am and returned to railhead (STEENWERK) and refilled. Returned to Nieppe.	A.9.1.D

121/5556

for
19th Bde Supply Coln

WAR DIARY

19th Inf Bde Supply Column

May - 1915.

Army Form C. 2118.

WAR DIARY
of
INTELLIGENCE SUMMARY 19th Inf Bde Supply Col.

(Erase heading not required.)

Instructions regarding War Diaries and Intelligence Summaries are contained in F. S. Regs, Part II. and the Staff Manual respectively. Title pages will be prepared in manuscript.

Hour, Date, Place	Summary of Events and Information	Remarks and references to Appendices
1st May 1915 — Nieppe.	Proceeded to refilling point at cross roads near railway crossing near Pont de Nieppe; dumped at 7.25am and returned to railhead (STEENWERK) and refilled. 2 Blacksmiths joined the Column from the BASE	A.9.1.D
2nd May 1915 — Nieppe.	Proceeded to refilling point at crossroads near railway crossing near Pont de Nieppe; dumped at 7.10am and returned to railhead (STEENWERK) and refilled.	A.9.1.D
3rd May 1915 — Nieppe.	Proceeded to refilling point at cross roads near railway crossing near Pont de Nieppe, dumped at 7.15am and returned to railhead (STEENWERK) and refilled.	A.9.1.D
4th May 1915 — Nieppe.	Proceeded to ERQUINGHAM, dumped at 7.35am, returned to railhead + refilled.	A.9.1.D

Army Form C. 2118.

WAR DIARY
of
INTELLIGENCE SUMMARY 19th Inf. Bde. Supply Column.

(Erase heading not required.)

Instructions regarding War Diaries and Intelligence Summaries are contained in F. S. Regs., Part II. and the Staff Manual respectively. Title pages will be prepared in manuscript.

Hour, Date, Place	Summary of Events and Information	Remarks and references to Appendices
5th May 1915 — Nieppe.	Dumped at ERQUINGHAM at 1.20 a.m. Returned to railhead (STEENWERK) and refilled.	A.9.1.C
6th May 1915 — Nieppe.	Dumped at ERQUINGHAM at 7.30 a.m. Returned to railhead (STEENWERK). The Train did not arrive until 2.55 p.m.	A.9.1.C
7th May 1915 — Nieppe.	Dumped at ERQUINGHAM; returned to railhead (STEENWERK) and refilled. 1 loader jorried from (6th Div. Supply Col.)	A.9.1.C
8th May 1915 — Nieppe.	Dumped at ERQUINGHAM, returned to railhead (STEENWERK) and refilled.	

Army Form C. 2118.

WAR DIARY
or
INTELLIGENCE SUMMARY   19th Inf. Bde. Supply Co.

(Erase heading not required.)

Instructions regarding War Diaries and Intelligence Summaries are contained in F. S. Regs., Part II. and the Staff Manual respectively. Title pages will be prepared in manuscript.

Hour, Date, Place	Summary of Events and Information	Remarks and references to Appendices
9th May 1915 --- Nieppe.	Proceeded to ERQUINGHAM; dumped and returned to railhead (STEENWERK) and refilled. Two 10th Sec'n Trains come in the day previous.	A9/D
10th May 1915 --- Nieppe	Proceeded to ERQUINGHAM, dumped and returned to railhead (STEENWERK) and refilled. 1 Blacksmith joined from the Base.	A9/D
11th May 1915 --- Nieppe	Proceeded to ERQUINGHAM; dumped and returned to railhead (STEENWERK) and refilled. two disinfectants carts on the 10th Sec'n Train.	A9/D
12th May 1915 --- Nieppe	Proceeded to ERQUINGHAM; dumped and returned to railhead (STEENWERK) and refilled. two disinfect- carts on the 10th Sec'n Train.	A9/D

Army Form C. 2118.

WAR DIARY
INTELLIGENCE SUMMARY

19th Inf. Bde Supply Co.

(Erase heading not required.)

Hour, Date, Place	Summary of Events and Information	Remarks and references to Appendices
13th May 1915 — Nieppe	Proceeded to refilling point at ERQUINGHAM, dumped and returned to railhead (STEENWERK) and refilled. 1 Barrel of crude oil sent to refilling point.	19.1.C
14th May 1915 — Nieppe.	Proceeded to ERQUINGHAM and dumped and returned to railhead (STEENWERK) and refilled. Daimler car broke down.	19.1.C
15th May 1915 — Nieppe.	Proceeded to ERQUINGHAM, dumped and returned to railhead (STEENWERK) and refilled. Three men reported sick, but none admitted to hospital	19.1.C
16th May 1915 — Nieppe.	Proceeded to ERQUINGHAM, dumped and returned to railhead (STEENWERK) and refilled. 1 Wheeler joined	19.1.C

WAR DIARY
INTELLIGENCE SUMMARY
19th Inf. Bde. Supply Col.

Army Form C. 2118.

(Erase heading not required.)

Hour, Date, Place	Summary of Events and Information	Remarks and references to Appendices
17th May 1915 — Nieppe.	Proceeded to ERQUINGHAM and dumped, returned to railhead (STEENWERK) and refilled.	19.1.C
18th May 1915 — Nieppe.	Proceeded to ERQUINGHAM and dumped, returned to railhead (STEENWERK) and refilled.	19.1.C
19th May 1915 — Nieppe.	Proceeded to ERQUINGHAM and dumped, returned to railhead (STEENWERK) and refilled. Lorry went at 1pm to Bde HQrs on duty.	19.1.C
20th May 1915 — Armentières.	Proceeded to ERQUINGHAM and dumped at 7.35am, returned to railhead (STEENWERK) and refilled. Dumped at ERQUINGHAM at 2.30pm; after which the Column proceeded to ARMENTIERES where it remained in new billets. Lorry on duty with BDE HQrs.	19.1.C
21st May 1915 — Armentières	Proceeded to railhead (STEENWERK) and refilled. 1 Lorry on duty with Bde HQrs	19.1.C

Army Form C. 2118.

WAR DIARY
of
INTELLIGENCE SUMMARY   19th Inf. Bde. Supply Col.

(Erase heading not required.)

Instructions regarding War Diaries and Intelligence Summaries are contained in F. S. Regs., Part II. and the Staff Manual respectively. Title pages will be prepared in manuscript.

Hour, Date, Place	Summary of Events and Information	Remarks and references to Appendices
22nd May 1915 --- Armentières	Dumped at ERQUINGHAM, returned to railhead (STEENWERK) and refilled. Pte Cassini transferred to 6th Div. Supply Col.	A.9.1.D
23rd May 1915 --- Armentières	Dumped at ERQUINGHAM, returned to railhead (STEENWERK) and refilled. Four drivers - 1 wheeler and 1 fitter joined from the BASE.	A.9.1.D
24th May 1915 --- Armentières.	Dumped at ERQUINGHAM, returned to railhead (STEENWERK) and refilled.	A.9.1.D
25th May 1915 --- Armentières.	Dumped at ERQUINGHAM, returned to railhead (STEENWERK) and refilled. Lorry no 4 taken down & released.	A.9.1.D
26th May 1915 --- Armentières.	Dumped at ERQUINGHAM, returned to railhead (STEENWERK) and refilled.	A.9.1.D

Army Form C. 2118.

WAR DIARY
or
INTELLIGENCE SUMMARY 10th In/Bde Supply Col

(Erase heading not required.)

Instructions regarding War Diaries and Intelligence Summaries are contained in F. S. Regs., Part II. and the Staff Manual respectively. Title pages will be prepared in manuscript.

Hour, Date, Place	Summary of Events and Information	Remarks and references to Appendices
27th May 1915 — Armentières	Dumped at ERQUINGHEM; returned to railhead (STEENWERK) and refilled. 1 Lorry lent to 6th Div. Hqrs.	A.9.1.D
28th May 1915 — Armentières	Dumped at ERQUINGHEM, returned to railhead (STEENWERK) and refilled. Sgt Jameson transferred to A.C's Office 8.H.Q. 1 Driver joined from 6th Div. Supply Col.	A.9.1.D
29th May 1915 — Armentières	Dumped at ERQUINGHEM; returned to railhead (STEENWERK) and refilled.	A.9.1.D
30th May 1915 — Armentières	Dumped at ERQUINGHEM; returned to railhead (STEENWERK) and refilled.	A.9.1.D
31st May 1915 — Armentières	Dumped at ERQUINGHEM, returned to railhead (STEENWERK) and refilled. 1 Lorry proceeded to POPERINGHE on duty with 6th Div.	A.9.1.D

1247 W 3290 200,000 (E) 8/14 J.B.C. & A. Forms/C. 2118/11.

27TH DIVISION
19TH INFY BDE

19TH BDE SUPPLY COLN.
JUN-JLY 1915

12/5935

19th Brigade

C of C

19th Bde Supply Coln
Vt XL

Army Form C. 2118

June 1915

WAR DIARY
or
INTELLIGENCE SUMMARY

(Erase heading not required.)

Instructions regarding War Diaries and Intelligence Summaries are contained in F. S. Regs., Part II. and the Staff Manual respectively. Title Pages will be prepared in manuscript.

19th Inf. Bde. Supply Column

Place	Date	Hour	Summary of Events and Information	Remarks and references to Appendices

Army Form C. 2118.

WAR DIARY
or
INTELLIGENCE SUMMARY

19th Bde Supply Col.

(Erase heading not required.)

Instructions regarding War Diaries and Intelligence Summaries are contained in F. S. Regs., Part II. and the Staff Manual respectively. Title pages will be prepared in manuscript.

Hour, Date, Place	Summary of Events and Information	Remarks and references to Appendices
1st June 1915 — Armentières	Dumped at ERQUINGHEM, returned to railhead (STEENWERK) refilled and returned to Armentières.	A.9.1.D
2nd June 1915 — Armentières	Dumped at ERQUINGHEM, returned to railhead (STEENWERK) and refilled.	A.9.1.D
3rd June 1915 — Armentières	Dumped at ERQUINGHEM, returned to railhead (STEENWERK) refilled. 1 Supply Clerk arrived from BASE. 1 Sergt proceeded to 16th Inf. Bde Store and returned stores to Train Store.	A.9.1.D
4th June 1915 — Armentières	Dumped at ERQUINGHEM; returned to railhead (STEENWERK) refilled.	A.9.1.D
5th June 1915 — Armentières	Dumped at ERQUINGHEM; returned to railhead (STEENWERK) and refilled.	A.9.1.D

WAR DIARY
or
INTELLIGENCE SUMMARY [of Hq Robt. Buckley Col.]

Army Form C. 2118.

(Erase heading not required.)

Hour, Date, Place	Summary of Events and Information	Remarks and references to Appendices
6th June 1915 — Armentières	Dumped at ERQUINGHEM, returned to railhead (STEENWERK) and refilled. Commer lorry no 1 broke a rear axle.	A.S.C.
7th June 1915 — Armentières	Dumped at ERQUINGHEM, returned to railhead (STEENWERK) and refilled.	A.S.C.
8th June 1915 — Armentières	Dumped at ERQUINGHEM, returned to railhead (STEENWERK) and refilled. Went to railhead at 7.30pm for 138 lbs Sugar deficient.	A.S.C.
9th June 1915 — Armentières	Dumped at ERQUINGHEM, returned to railhead (STEENWERK) and refilled.	A.S.C.
10th June 1915 — Armentières	Dumped at ERQUINGHEM, returned to railhead (STEENWERK) and refilled.	A.S.C.
11th June 1915 — Armentières	Dumped at ERQUINGHEM, returned to railhead (STEENWERK) and refilled.	A.S.C.

Army Form C. 2118.

WAR DIARY

INTELLIGENCE SUMMARY 19th Inf Bde Supply Col.

(Erase heading not required.)

Instructions regarding War Diaries and Intelligence Summaries are contained in F. S. Regs, Part II. and the Staff Manual respectively. Title pages will be prepared in manuscript.

Hour, Date, Place	Summary of Events and Information	Remarks and references to Appendices
12th June 1915 — Armentières	Proceeded to ERQUINGHEM, dumped and returned to railhead (STEENWERK) and refilled.	A.S.C.
13th June 1915 — Armentières	Proceeded to ERQUINGHEM, dumped and returned to railhead (STEENWERK) and refilled	A.S.C.
14th June 1915 — Armentières	Proceeded to ERQUINGHEM, dumped and returned to railhead (STEENWERK) and refilled. Pte STAW despatched to the BASE.	A.S.C.
15th June 1915 — Armentières	Proceeded to ERQUINGHEM; dumped and returned to railhead (STEENWERK) and refilled. 1 Lorry to NIEPPE for pickets.	A.S.C.
16th June 1915 — Armentières	Proceeded to ERQUINGHEM; dumped and returned to railhead (STEENWERK) and refilled. 1 Lorry proceeded to the FOREST of NIEPPE. 1 Lorry sent to IJSEBERGUES to be retyred. 160 Sks sugar fetched from WARDRECQUES by car.	A.S.C.
17th June 1915 — Armentières	Proceeded to ERQUINGHEM, dumped and returned to railhead (STEENWERK) and refilled.	A.S.C.

Army Form C. 2118.

WAR DIARY
of
INTELLIGENCE SUMMARY 19th Inf. Bde. Supply Col.

(Erase heading not required.)

Instructions regarding War Diaries and Intelligence Summaries are contained in F. S. Regs., Part II. and the Staff Manual respectively. Title pages will be prepared in manuscript.

Hour, Date, Place	Summary of Events and Information	Remarks and references to Appendices
18th June 1915 — Armentières.	Dumped at ERQUINGHEM, returned to railhead (STEENWERK) and refilled. Soon proceeded to FOREST of NIEPPE for tickets.	A.F.S.C.
19th June 1915 — Armentières.	Dumped at ERQUINGHEM, returned to railhead (STEENWERK) and refilled. M.S.S. Skelton proceeded on leave.	A.F.S.C.
20th June 1915 — Armentières.	Dumped at ERQUINGHEM; returned to railhead (STEENWERK) and refilled.	A.F.S.C.
21st June 1915 — Armentières.	Dumped at ERQUINGHEM; returned to railhead (STEENWERK) and refilled.	A.F.S.C.
22nd June 1915 — Armentières.	Dumped at ERQUINGHEM, returned to railhead (STEENWERK) and refilled. Advanced M.T. Depot sent up a back axle complete, instead of model W.P. R.C. instead of model	A.F.S.C.

Army Form C. 2118.

WAR DIARY
of INTELLIGENCE SUMMARY 19th Ind. Bde. Supply Col.

(Erase heading not required.)

Instructions regarding War Diaries and Intelligence Summaries are contained in F. S. Regs., Part II. and the Staff Manual respectively. Title pages will be prepared in manuscript.

Hour, Date, Place	Summary of Events and Information	Remarks and references to Appendices
23rd June 1915 — Armentières.	Dumped at ERQUINGHEM, returned to railhead (STEENWERK) and refilled.	A.9.1.D
24th June 1915 — Armentières.	Dumped at ERQUINGHEM, returned to railhead (STEENWERK) and refilled.	A.9.1.D
25th June 1915 — Armentières.	Dumped at ERQUING HEM, returned to railhead (STEENWERK) and refilled. Store car broke down.	A.9.1.D
26th June 1915 — Armentières.	Dumped at ERQUINGHEM, returned to railhead (STEENWERK) and refilled.	A.9.1.D
27th June 1915 — Armentières.	Dumped at ERQUINGHEM, returned to railhead (STEENWERK) and refilled.	A.9.1.D
28th June 1915 — Armentières.	Dumped at ERQUINGHEM, returned to railhead (STEENWERK) and refilled.	A.9.1.D

WAR DIARY
of
INTELLIGENCE SUMMARY 19th Inf Bde Supply Col.

Army Form C. 2118

(Erase heading not required.)

Instructions regarding War Diaries and Intelligence Summaries are contained in F. S. Regs., Part II. and the Staff Manual respectively. Title Pages will be prepared in manuscript.

Place	Date	Hour	Summary of Events and Information	Remarks and references to Appendices
Armentières	29. June		Dumped at ERQUINGHEM, returned to railhead (STEENWERK) at 9 am refilled and returned to Armentières.	#92. D
Armentières	30. June		Dumped at ERQUINGHEM, returned to railhead (STEENWERK) and refilled.	#91. D

121/6273

23rd Brigade
—
L of C

19th Brigade Supply Col
Vol XII

Army Form C. 2118

WAR DIARY
or
INTELLIGENCE SUMMARY JULY

(Erase heading not required.)

Instructions regarding War Diaries and Intelligence Summaries are contained in F.S. Regs., Part II. and the Staff Manual respectively. Title Pages will be prepared in manuscript.

Place	Date	Hour	Summary of Events and Information	Remarks and references to Appendices
			War Diary of 19th Inf. Bde. Supply Column	

WAR DIARY of INTELLIGENCE SUMMARY

Army Form C. 2118

(Erase heading not required.)

Place	Date	Hour	Summary of Events and Information	Remarks and references to Appendices
Armentières.	July 1st 1915		Proceeded to ERQUINGHAM, dumped and returned to railhead (STEENWERK) and refilled.	A.9.D
Armentières.	July 2nd 1915		Proceeded to ERQUINGHAM, dumped and returned to railhead (STEENWERK) and refilled. 1 Lorry proceeded to the FORÊT de NIEPPE to fetch packets.	A.9.D
Armentières.	July 3rd 1915		Proceeded to ERQUINGHAM, dumped and returned to railhead (STEENWERK) and refilled. Sgt-Cross went on leave.	A.9.D
Armentières	July 4th		Proceeded to ERQUINGHEM, dumped, returned to railhead (STEENWERK) and refilled.	A.9.D
Armentières	July 5th		Proceeded to ERQUINGHEM, dumped and returned to railhead (STEENWERK) and refilled.	A.9.D
Armentières	July 6th		Proceeded to ERQUINGHEM, dumped and returned to railhead (STEENWERK) and refilled. Pte Radford went on leave.	A.9.D
Armentières	July 7th		Proceeded to ERQUINGHEM, dumped and returned to railhead (STEENWERK)	A.9.D

Army Form C. 2118

WAR DIARY
of
INTELLIGENCE SUMMARY 10th Inf. Bde. Supply Col.

(Erase heading not required.)

Instructions regarding War Diaries and Intelligence Summaries are contained in F.S. Regs., Part II. and the Staff Manual respectively. Title Pages will be prepared in manuscript.

Place	Date	Hour	Summary of Events and Information	Remarks and references to Appendices
Armentières	July 8th/15	8.0.	Proceeded to ERQUINGHEM, dumped and returned to railhead (STEENWERK) and refilled. Frozen meat came up in an Insulated truck for the first time.	A.9.1.D
Armentières	July 9th	9.0.	Proceeded to ERQUINGHEM, dumped and returned to railhead (STEENWERK) and refilled. Sgt Cross returned off leave.	A.9.1.D
Armentières	July 10th	10.0.	Proceeded to ERQUINGHEM, dumped and returned to railhead (STEENWERK) and refilled.	A.9.1.D
Armentières	July 11th	8.0.	Proceeded to ERQUINGHEM, dumped and returned to railhead (STEENWERK) and refilled. Lorries inspected by Major Coulson.	A.9.1.D
Armentières	July 12th		Proceeded to ERQUINGHEM, dumped and returned to railhead (STEENWERK) and refilled.	A.9.1.D
Armentières	July 13th		Proceeded to ERQUINGHEM, dumped and returned to railhead (STEENWERK) and refilled. Cpl. Brockwel went on leave.	A.9.1.D

WAR DIARY
or
INTELLIGENCE SUMMARY

10th Inf. Bde. Supply Col.

Army Form C. 2118

(Erase heading not required.)

Place	Date	Hour	Summary of Events and Information	Remarks and references to Appendices
Armentieres.	July 14th.		Proceeded to ERQUINGHEM, dumped and returned to railhead (STEENWERK) and refilled.	A.R.I.D
STEENWERK (Armentieres)	July 15th.		Proceeded to ERQUINGHEM, dumped and returned to railhead (STEENWERK) and refilled. The Column moved to STEENWERK.	A.R.I.D
STEENWERK.	July 16th.		Proceeded to ERQUINGHEM, dumped and returned to railhead (STEENWERK) and refilled.	A.R.I.D
STEENWERK	July 17th.		Proceeded to ERQUINGHEM, dumped and returned to railhead (STEENWERK) and refilled.	A.R.I.D
STEENWERK	July 18th.		Proceeded to cross roads S.W. of CROIX de BAC, dumped and proceeded to railhead LA GORGUE, refilled at 12.30 p.m. and returned to STEENWERK.	A.R.I.D
STEENWERK	July 19th.		Proceeded to cross roads S.W. of CROIX de BAC, dumped and proceeded to railhead LA GORGUE, refilled and returned to STEENWERK.	A.R.I.D

WAR DIARY
or
INTELLIGENCE SUMMARY 19th Inf. Bde. Supply Col.

(Erase heading not required.)

Army Form C. 2118

Place	Date	Hour	Summary of Events and Information	Remarks and references to Appendices
Steenwerk	July 20th 1915		Dumped at cross roads ½ mile SW of Croix de Bac, proceeded to railhead La Gorgue refilled and returned to Steenwerk. Lorry sent to Base.	A.9.1.D
Steenwerk	July 21st 1915		Dumped at cross roads 400x S of Steenwerk, proceeded to railhead La Gorgue, refilled and returned to Steenwerk.	A.9.1.D
8th Doulieu	July 22nd 1915		Dumped at cross roads 400x S of Steenwerk, proceeded to railhead La Gorgue refilled and moved to Doulieu.	A.9.1.D
Doulieu	July 23rd 1915.		Dumped at cross roads at Le Nouveau Monde, refilled at railhead, La Gorgue and returned to Doulieu. DDST & 1st Orwel inspected the Column.	A.9.1.D
Doulieu	July 24th 1915.		Dumped at cross roads at Le Nouveau Monde, refilled at railhead, La Gorgue, and returned to Doulieu.	A.9.1.D
Doulieu	July 25th 1915		Dumped at cross roads at Le Nouveau Monde, refilled at railhead La Gorgue and returned to Doulieu.	A.9.1.D

1875 Wt. W593/S26 1,000,000 4/15 J.B.C. & A. A.D.S.S./Forms/C. 2118.

WAR DIARY

INTELLIGENCE SUMMARY 19th Inf. Bde Supply Col.

Army Form C. 2118

Instructions regarding War Diaries and Intelligence Summaries are contained in F.S. Regs., Part II. and the Staff Manual respectively. Title Pages will be prepared in manuscript.

(Erase heading not required.)

Place	Date	Hour	Summary of Events and Information	Remarks and references to Appendices
Doulieu.	July 26th 1915.		Dumped at Le Nouveau Monde, proceeded to Thiennes, refilled and returned to Doulieu.	A.9.1.D
Doulieu.	July 27th 1915.		Proceeded to Le Nouveau Monde and dumped. Refilled at Thiennes and returned to Doulieu. L. Cpl Nicholson returned off leave. Pte Cooper proceeded on leave.	A.9.1.D
Doulieu.	July 28th 1915.		Dumped at Le Nouveau Monde and dumped. Refilled at Thiennes, drew sleeve from the hangars at Aire; returned to Doulieu.	A.9.1.D
Doulieu.	July 29th 1915.		Dumped at Le Nouveau Monde, refilled at La Gorgue. Detached 1.3 Ton Commer lorry from D.D.H.S + T. 1st Army.	A.9.1.D
Doulieu.	July 30th 1915.		Dumped at Le Nouveau Monde, refilled at La Gorgue and returned to Doulieu.	A.9.1.D
Doulieu.	July 31st 1915		Dumped at Le Nouveau Monde, refilled at La Gorgue and returned to Doulieu. Took A.F.B.213 to DD & T. 1st Army in the afternoon.	A.9.1.D

1875 Wt. W593/826 1,000,000 4/15 J.B.C. & A. A.D.S.S./Forms/C. 2118.

19th Brigade.

G L of C

19th Brigade Supply Col"

Vol XIII

From 1st to 30th August 1915

D/6508

Army Form C. 2118

WAR DIARY
of 19th Inf. Bde. Supply Col.
INTELLIGENCE SUMMARY

(Erase heading not required.)

August

Place	Date	Hour	Summary of Events and Information	Remarks and references to Appendices
Doulieu.	1-8-15	—	Dumped at Le Nouveau Monde; refilled at La Gorgue and returned to Doulieu. H.S.N. Shallow proceeded to Havre for duty with his Cruives. Date of promotion 27-7-15. Authority ASC/507/32.	A91.C
Doulieu.	2-8-15	—	Dumped at Le Nouveau Monde; refilled at La Gorgue and returned to Doulieu. Pte Cooper returned from leave. Sitter Dougie awarded 21 days Field Punishment No 1	A91.C
Doulieu.	3-8-15	—	Dumped at Le Nouveau Monde; refilled at La Gorgue and returned to Doulieu.	A91.C
Doulieu.	4-8-15	—	Dumped at Le Nouveau Monde; refilled at La Gorgue and returned to Doulieu.	A91.C
Doulieu.	5-8-15	—	Dumped at Le Nouveau Monde; refilled at La Gorgue and returned to Doulieu. No meat or bread came up on the train.	A91.C
Doulieu.	6-8-15	—	Dumped at Le Nouveau Monde, refilled at La Gorgue and returned to Doulieu. Bread and meat dumped the same morning as drawn.	A91.C

WAR DIARY
or
INTELLIGENCE SUMMARY 19th Inf. Bde Supply Col.

(Erase heading not required.)

Army Form C. 2118

Place	Date	Hour	Summary of Events and Information	Remarks and references to Appendices
DOULIEU	7.8.15	—	Dumped at LE NOUVEAU MONDE, returned to railhead LA GORGUE and refilled. Capt. Danbury proceeded on leave. Motor cyclist broke down near Merville.	J.T.
DOULIEU	8.8.15	—	Proceeded to LE NOUVEAU MONDE and dumped; returned to railhead LA GORGUE and refilled. Sgt. fitter FRY proceeded on leave.	J.T.
DOULIEU	9.8.15	—	Proceeded to LE NOUVEAU MONDE, dumped returned to railhead LAGORGUE and refilled. Sovy proceeded to G.H.Q with old motor cycle & magneto.	J.T.
DOULIEU	10.8.15	—	Dumped at LE NOUVEAU MONDE; returned to railhead LA GORGUE and refilled.	J.T.
DOULIEU	11.8.15	.	Dumped at LE NOUVEAU MONDE; returned to railhead, LA GORGUE and refilled.	J.T.
DOULIEU	12.8.15		Dumped at LE NOUVEAU MONDE; returned to railhead, LA GORGUE and refilled. Morning parade altered from 7am to 6.45 am.	J.T.

WAR DIARY
INTELLIGENCE SUMMARY 10th Inf Bde Supply Col.

Army Form C. 2118

(Erase heading not required.)

Instructions regarding War Diaries and Intelligence Summaries are contained in F.S. Regs., Part II. and the Staff Manual respectively. Title Pages will be prepared in manuscript.

Place	Date	Hour	Summary of Events and Information	Remarks and references to Appendices
DOULIEU	13.8.15	—	Proceeded to LE NOUVEAU MONDE, dumped and returned to railhead LA GORGUE and refilled. H.Qrs Car returned overhauled.	I.T.
DOULIEU	14.8.15	—	Proceeded to LE NOUVEAU MONDE, dumped and returned to railhead LA GORGUE and refilled. S' Taylor proceeded to D.D of S.T. 1st Army with A.F.B 213 A.]	I.T.
DOULIEU	15.8.15	—	Dumped at LE NOUVEAU MONDE, returned to railhead LA GORGUE and refilled. Capt. Daubeny returned from leave.	I.T.
DOULIEU	16.8.15	—	Dumped 1 mile N.E of ESTAIRES, returned to railhead LA GORGUE and refilled.	4.91.0
DOULIEU	17.8.15	—	Dumped 1 mile N.E of ESTAIRES, returned to railhead LA GORGUE and refilled.	4.91.0
DOULIEU	18.8.15	—	Dumped 1 mile N.E of ESTAIRES, returned to railhead LA GORGUE and refilled with groceries and forage for 4th Guards Bde. Column moved to ST MARTIN. (ST OMER)	4.91.0

Army Form C. 2118

WAR DIARY
or
INTELLIGENCE SUMMARY 19th Sup. Boe Supply Col

(Erase heading not required.)

Instructions regarding War Diaries and Intelligence Summaries are contained in F. S. Regs., Part II. and the Staff Manual respectively. Title Pages will be prepared in manuscript.

Place	Date	Hour	Summary of Events and Information	Remarks and references to Appendices
ST OMER.	19.8.15		Proceeded to St Marie after having filled up with Bread & meat, dumped for the 4th Guards Bde.	A.9.1.D
ST OMER.	20.8.15		Handed over the column to the Guards Divisional Supply Col.	A.9.1.D

www.ingramcontent.com/pod-product-compliance
Lightning Source LLC
Chambersburg PA
CBHW081439160426
43193CB00013B/2332